POSITIVE BEHAVIOR
Activities for Kids

AGES 4–8

POSITIVE BEHAVIOR
Activities for Kids

50 Fun and Engaging Exercises to Help Kids
Make Good Choices at Home, at School, and Beyond

STACY SPENSLEY

ILLUSTRATIONS BY ELZBIETA SMIETANKA-COMBIK

CALLISTO PUBLISHING

Published by Callisto Publishing LLC C/O Sourcebooks LLC

P.O. Box 4410, Naperville, Illinois 60567-4410

(630) 961-3900

callistopublishing.com

This product conforms to all applicable CPSC and CPSIA standards.

Source of Production: 1010 Printing Asia Limited, Kwun Tong, Hong Kong, China

Date of Production: August 2023

Run Number: SBCAL62

Printed and bound in China.

1010 14

TO IVER, RYKER, AND CLARA
FOR BEING MY BEST
TEACHERS AND TEST SUBJECTS.

AND ANDERSON
FOR HIS UNWAVERING SUPPORT.

CONTENTS

A NOTE FOR CAREGIVERS

Welcome! If you've purchased this book, it's probably because you want to encourage positive behavior in children, whether they're related to you or somehow in your care. You may be struggling with challenging behavior or out of tools that are working for you. It's easy to feel like you're failing, and you may be getting advice that you need to discipline harder, or "make" a child behave better. If only it worked that way! You're not failing, and you're not alone. I'm grateful you're looking for positive ways to address these challenges.

The two mantras I try to remember are "all behavior is communication" and "children do well when they can." These ideas are the foundation of the activities in this book. If kids are struggling, it's because some need isn't being met, even if we can't see it yet. The activities, games, and exercises that follow seek to address those invisible needs. Maybe their body is dysregulated so they can't access tools for calming down or managing their emotions. Maybe they need connection. Perhaps they need a more robust vocabulary for communicating how they feel.

There are no "bad" kids, so if you're raising or working with a child whose behavior is challenging, remember it's not fun for them to feel that way either. With this book, I want to provide a shared language for children and caregivers to discuss big feelings in a respectful and positive way. Shaming and punishing kids for being human doesn't help anyone. If adults were perfect at controlling their feelings, we wouldn't have online comments or road rage! Expecting more of people who have decades less life experience sets everyone up for disappointment.

This book is written for preschoolers and up, but these exercises can also help you. Many of us were taught that expressing our feelings was "bad" or were even punished for crying or being angry. If those were the lessons we learned, it can be a challenge to hold space for kids to express the feelings that we weren't allowed to express.

The book is aimed at kids between four and eight years old. Younger children or those who can't read and write will need more help, but older kids should be able to use the book on their own if they want. The activities will help kids build a stronger emotional vocabulary, learn strategies and practices to strengthen their self-regulation, discover methods for calming down, develop empathy for others, and improve their cooperation skills. Not everything will apply to every child because not everyone has siblings or goes to school, but I hope each task provides a jumping-off point for discussion and engagement.

My own kids are currently eight, four, and two, and I use many of these strategies in our home regularly. All kids have sensory needs, but many of these activities are particularly helpful for kids (like mine) with sensory processing challenges, ADHD, or other neurodiversity. ("Neurodiversity" describes people who are autistic or have ADHD, OCD, anxiety, Tourette's, dyslexia, etc. Neurodiverse kids can have unique behavior challenges because of how their brains interpret and express information.)

INTRODUCTION

Hello, readers! Whether you're a kid or a grown-up, I hope you enjoy this book and the fun activities inside. The goal of the book is to improve behavior, but I know when grown-ups say that, it usually means they want you to do what they say. That's not what this book is about. When I talk about behavior, I mean the way you act based on how you feel.

There Are No Bad Feelings!

This book talks a lot about feelings, but always remember that no feelings are bad. We all have feelings, and that's a normal part of being human. Even grown-ups have a hard time with strong feelings sometimes, and we've had more practice! I hope this book gives you new ideas for naming, experiencing, and acting on those feelings. Whether you're having small feelings or big ones, feelings don't last forever.

There Are No Bad Kids, But Some Behaviors Are Not Okay

It's also important to remember you're not a "bad" kid just because you have strong feelings. If those feelings make you so mad that you want to hit, that's totally normal, but it doesn't make it okay to hit someone. If you do, it's important to calm your body down and apologize.

Activities Can Help

This book is full of activities that can help you with your feelings. Some will show you how to identify your feelings by talking about them. You might discover that you need to practice calming your body down before you're so upset that you hurt someone. Sometimes, you may get so upset that you need help calming down, and that's good information to have.

Other activities will show you why you might be feeling a certain way. For example, maybe you get angry more often when you're hungry or tired.

There are also activities that help you identify what makes you feel happy and excited and joyful!

Drawing, Writing, Playing, and Imagining

Some activities invite you to draw or write in this book. Others are games or physical activities, arts and crafts projects, or ways to use your imagination. You can start at the beginning or skip around to specific pages. You might need a grown-up to help you with some projects and reading directions, but others you can do on your own.

Just try one and see how it works for you. Some you might do only one time; others you might do regularly. You may need help relaxing your body, calming down your mind, seeing a situation from another point of view, or even falling asleep at night.

The Chapters

The 50 activities in this book are divided into three chapters:

- **Chapter 1: Little Things**—everyday activities that help you name and understand your feelings, learn how to stay calm, and move around in helpful ways
- **Chapter 2: Getting Along**—games and activities that help you understand and care about other people's feelings and give you a chance to practice being with others
- **Chapter 3: Big Feelings**—tools and plans for helping you handle your strong feelings

Our Favorites

I have three kids at home, and my husband and I use most of these activities with them. If you need a place to start, my kids especially like making Bubble Mountains (page 11), Glitter Jars (page 88), and Mandalas (page 40), and we do a daily Goodnight Gratitude (page 29) list. I'm grateful for all of you for reading this book!

CHAPTER 1

Little Things

Every day, we make lots of small choices. We decide what to eat for breakfast, what clothes to wear, what books to read, and what music to listen to. We also decide how to treat other people, who to play with, and how to express ourselves. The activities in this chapter will help you with the feelings that come up as a part of your everyday life. Some are meant to become daily habits; others are fun when you want to try something new or helpful when what you've been doing isn't working anymore.

There are morning activities and bedtime activities, drawing and coloring activities, games to move your body, and ways to understand your emotions. I hope you find new ways to talk about feelings and deal with any that come up. Remember that feelings aren't good or bad, and they will pass. What will you try first?

My Morning Routine

A routine is simply a set of things we do all the time. You might already have a routine without knowing it. Having a routine helps us remember everything we need to do in order, step by step. A routine can be very useful to keep you moving forward in the morning so you can get ready with less help from a grown-up. If everyone is rushing around, it's easy for things to be forgotten.

In this activity, you'll write down a morning routine so you don't forget any of the steps. Then you'll find a place to post your list. This list will help you be responsible for getting yourself ready in the morning so the day will go more smoothly.

Part of the activity is figuring out what works, so it may take a few tries to get it right—and that's okay! Some people may want to brush their teeth before getting dressed, and some might want to get dressed before breakfast. See what works best for you.

What You'll Need

- A computer and printer (ask a grown-up to help)
- A piece of paper and pen (if you don't have a computer and printer)
- Colored pencils or markers

MORNING ROUTINE

- Wake up
- Eat breakfast
- Brush teeth
- Get dressed
- Put on shoes
- Leave for school

Directions

1. Write down or type what you do every morning, in order. Do you eat the same thing for breakfast each day? Do you need to pack your lunch or bring a snack? Do you take a shower?

2. Print out your list if you're using a computer. Add colors or drawings if you want. It can help to add pictures if you can't read by yourself yet. Hang up your routine where you can see it, preferably near where you do most of these things. Is that in your room, by the table, or near the door?

3. In the morning, check your routine to see what order you do things in.

4. If something is missing, add it in! If you need a different routine for weekends, you might want to make two lists.

My Magic Morning Mantras

How do you feel when you wake up in the morning? Happy and rested? Tired and grumpy? Or somewhere in the middle?

No one is happy all the time because we all experience different feelings, and that's normal and okay. But sometimes, if we wake up in a bad mood, it can affect our whole day.

We can't always control how we feel, but we can control how we act. Before we even get out of bed, we can try using some magic phrases called mantras or affirmations. These are short sayings that focus on good things to help us improve our mood. When we remind ourselves of how we want to act, we're more likely to make positive choices that feel good for us and others. You might use a mantra on a day you're feeling especially grumpy to help improve your mood, or you can say these every morning to start each day on a positive note.

What You'll Need

- A pencil or pen

Directions

Pick a phrase from the list below, depending on what you need to hear. Say it when you first wake up in the morning or anytime during the day. You can even say it into the mirror for a huge mood boost!

- Today is a great day.

- I am happy, I am healthy, I am safe.

- I am loved.

- I love to learn.

- I'm a good friend.

- I can do anything I put my mind to.

- I believe in myself.

- I am giving.

- I do the best I can because no one is perfect.

- I am kind.

- I care about others and our planet.

Now write some mantras of your own!

I

I

I

I

Make a Mood Meter

Sometimes, when we're upset, it's hard to explain how we feel in words. We can create a Mood Meter to measure our feelings, just like a thermometer measures temperature, so we can talk about what's happening in our bodies.

Remember that feelings aren't good or bad, but strong feelings can make our brains unable to think straight. Parents can do this, too, since even adults have to deal with big feelings.

What You'll Need

- A piece of paper
- Colored pencils or markers

Directions

How to create your Mood Meter:

1. Use the illustration on the next page as an example or draw your own Mood Meter shape.

2. Choose a number scale. It could be 1 to 5 or 1 to 100. There's no wrong answer. The bigger the number, the bigger your mood. The example below uses a scale of 1 to 10, where 1 is happy and 10 is a meltdown. Your moods might need a bigger range, and that's okay.

3. Draw or write how you feel next to each number.

4. Talk about your scale so everyone understands what each number means for you.

5. Hang up your Mood Meter where you can see it.

How to use your Mood Meter:

1. Have a morning mood check where everyone shares their number. "I'm a 1 and I'm happy!" "I'm a 3 because I have a headache." "I'm a 6! Humph!"

2. When you're upset but can't figure out why, you can say what number your mood is to give people an idea of how you're feeling.

3. Think of ways to bring your number down. On a scale of 1 to 10, you can probably come up with some ways to calm yourself up to number 5, but you'll need help if you're at a 6 or higher.

4. Write down the ideas you come up with and name your list your Calm Down Menu. Use this menu the next time you're upset.

Mood Meter

10	MELTDOWN, EMERGENCY
9	FURIOUS (SCREAMING, CRYING)
8	ANGRIER (HITTING, KICKING))
7	ANGRY (FACE IS HOT, FISTS CLENCHED)
6	STOMACH FEELS TIGHT
5	FRUSTRATED, HARDER TO TALK
4	MORE ANNOYED (EYEBROWS ARE PULLED DOWN, FROWNING)
3	A LITTLE ANNOYED
2	STILL OKAY, BUT MAYBE BORED
1	CALM, HAPPY

Feelings Word Search

Feelings aren't good or bad, but they can sometimes seem that way. People might tell us it's not okay to be sad or angry. It can also be confusing when we don't quite know how to explain what we're feeling at the moment. This happens a lot with big feelings and can be overwhelming.

It can also be hard to describe how you feel if you don't have the word for that emotion. Happy, joyful, and proud are all warm feelings, but they're very different from each other! Frustrated, scared, and jealous are feelings we may not enjoy much, but each is different from the others.

Directions

Read through the list of feelings below and circle how many you have felt this week.

EXCITED ANGRY

HAPPY JEALOUS

SAD NERVOUS

GRUMPY

WORRIED SURPRISED

SCARED CURIOUS LONELY

LOVING BORED PEACEFUL

EMBARRASSED HOPEFUL

PROUD

Growing Your Garden of Feelings

Everyone gets sad and mad sometimes, but we'd rather feel more positive emotions when we can. We can't always control how we feel or the situations we're in, but we can take small actions over time to feel warm feelings. Our feelings are like seeds in a garden that need certain things to grow and flourish. How do we tend to our feelings garden? What actions do we take that make us happy?

When you plant a seed, you bury it in soil, water it, and give it sunlight. Then it sprouts and grows. Without all those things in place, the plant can't grow and bloom. Our moods can be the same way. Sometimes, you can be in a great mood, and then something happens and you're not anymore.

Directions

What feelings seeds do you want to plant, and what are the soil, water, and sunlight that keep them growing and happy? Complete the following sentence using one of the examples below or choose your own words.

The seed I want to grow is _____

and I will water it by _____

Examples:

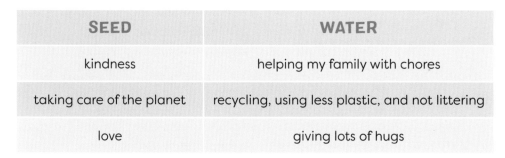

SEED	WATER
kindness	helping my family with chores
taking care of the planet	recycling, using less plastic, and not littering
love	giving lots of hugs

Bubble Mountain

This is a bubble activity you can do inside and in any weather. Try this out when you have a lot of energy in your body but not a lot of space to run around or make a lot of noise with your mouth, or when you have lots of thoughts in your head and can't focus on other things. See how it makes you feel.

What You'll Need

- A dish towel
- 1 cup of water
- A tall cup
- A few drops of hand soap or dish detergent
- A drinking straw

Directions

1. Place the towel on a flat surface to catch any spills.

2. Pour about 2 inches of water in the cup. Add the soap.

3. Put the straw in the cup and blow through the straw to create bubbles. The bubbles will foam up over the edge of the cup. See how tall you can make them! Be careful not to drink the soapy water. Ick!

4. Make sure you clean everything up when you're finished.

A Recipe for YOU!

Each of us is unique—that means one of a kind. And being different is what makes you YOU. There is no one else quite like you on earth, even if you have a twin!

Sometimes, when we see people who look or act different than us, it can seem strange at first, but if we were all exactly the same, that would be pretty boring. So, what are the things that make you different from everyone else?

A recipe is a list of ingredients that get mixed together to make something more than each item alone. If you heard you were going to eat flour, butter, sugar, and eggs, that's not very exciting. But you might feel differently if you found out that, together, those things made a cake!

No matter what you look like, what you're great at, or what you're not good at yet, you are more than any one of those things. So, let's make a list of "ingredients" that, together, make up wonderful, unique YOU.

Directions

For the You recipe:

1. Fill in the blanks below.

A RECIPE FOR _____ (fill in your name)

Ingredients:

- Skin color: _____
- Eye color: _____
- Hair color: _____
- Hair texture: _____
- Favorite color: _____
- Favorite animal: _____
- Favorite food: _____
- Favorite thing to play: _____
- Favorite book: _____
- Favorite thing about yourself: _____

- Something you're really good at: _____

- Something you feel most proud of: _____

- Something else you want people to know about you: _____

For making the recipe:

1. Pretend to put all the ingredients in a bowl and mix thoroughly.

2. Now draw a picture of yourself in the bowl.

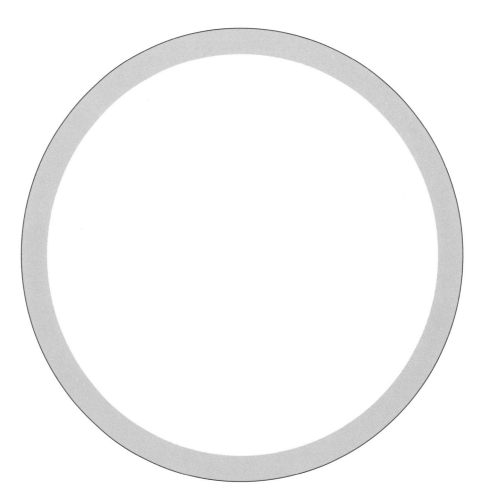

What Color Are My Feelings?

Not everyone has the same favorite color, and not everyone has the same color feelings! There are a few examples in this book about how to measure the strength of your feelings or name the different feelings you might have. Matching your feelings to a color is just one more way to tell people how you feel.

There are no right or wrong answers because you're the only one who knows how your body is feeling inside. You can use this chart to give grown-ups a secret code to understand how you feel. Sometimes you might even feel so upset that you can't talk, but you could point to the color on this page to express your emotion.

What You'll Need

- A piece of paper (if you want to hang up your drawing when you're finished)

- A pencil or pen

- Crayons, colored pencils, or paint and a paintbrush

Directions

1. For each circle, read the word (or have a grown-up read it to you), close your eyes, and picture what color that feeling looks like to you.

2. Color in the circle with that color.

3. Repeat for the other feelings.

4. Hang up the page if you want and use those colors to describe your mood if you have trouble coming up with the words.

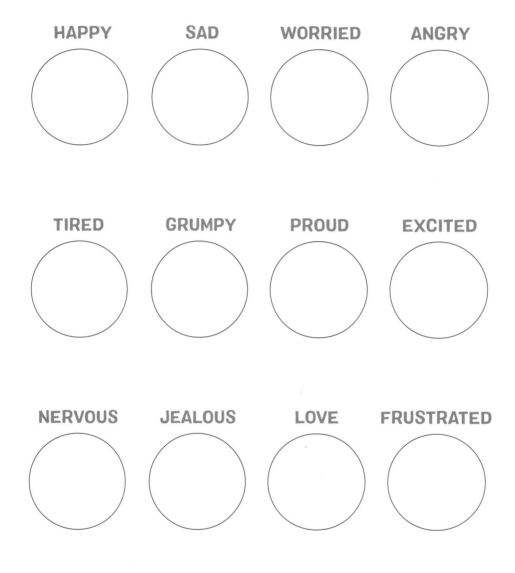

HAPPY

SAD

WORRIED

ANGRY

TIRED

GRUMPY

PROUD

EXCITED

NERVOUS

JEALOUS

LOVE

FRUSTRATED

What's in Your Worry Cloud?

When we're worried, it can feel like a big cloud of icky feelings is covering up the sun's rays of happiness. All those worries and fears stick together in your Worry Cloud. Your Worry Cloud can fill up your head so you can't think about anything else. You might not be able to concentrate, your head or tummy might hurt, or you might want to hit or throw things.

What if you could get your Worry Cloud to go away?

What You'll Need

- Crayons, colored pencils, or colored markers

Directions

1. In the cloud below, draw pictures or colors of your worries, or simply write them down in words. They might be things that start with "What if . . ."

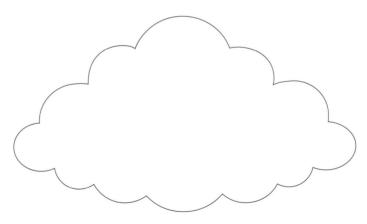

2. Once you've drawn all the worries you can think of, we want the Worry Cloud to leave! Close your eyes and picture it gone.

How did you get it to go away?

Did you shout, "Go away, Worry Cloud! I don't need you!"

Did you say, "Thank you, Worry Cloud, but you're not helping right now."

Did the sun come out and shine through the cloud?

Did you punch it into outer space?

Did you pretend to be a monster and scare the cloud away?

There's no wrong answer! In the box below, write or draw how you got rid of the Worry Cloud. Next time you feel stuck under a Worry Cloud, try chasing it away like that and see if it works.

Scented Squish Dough

Did you know that of our five senses, smell is the strongest? Our noses can remember 50,000 smells! That's everything from your favorite food to the stinkiest stench. Certain smells can also make us feel relaxed, more alert, or even sleepy. Pretty cool, huh?

This fun activity uses a lot of your senses! First, you can make the dough, then you can save it for later. Squishing the dough can help you get out some big feelings when you want to smash things, and the scent can help you calm down.

Or you can make wake-up dough for when you're having a hard time focusing. Squeezing and working with this dough helps warm up the muscles in your hands, and you can choose a scent and color that helps you be more alert. Be creative!

You can squeeze the dough before writing or doing other craft activities to wake up your fingers and make them stronger. It can help you sit still longer, too. If you're feeling upset, you can roll the dough into a ball to smash.

What You'll Need

- A grown-up (to help with the stove and essential oils)
- 2 cups all-purpose flour
- ¾ cup salt
- 4 teaspoons cream of tartar
- 2 cups lukewarm water
- 2 tablespoons coconut or vegetable oil
- Food coloring (optional)
- Essential oils (See some suggestions for oils and the Safety Note to Grown-ups on the next page.)

Directions

1. Combine the flour, salt, and cream of tartar in a medium saucepan.

2. Add the water and oil. If you're making one color, add the food coloring now, too.

3. Cook over medium heat, stirring constantly, until the dough thickens and forms a ball.

4. Let the mixture cool and divide it into batches. Add the food coloring if you're making more than one color.

5. Add 1 to 2 drops of essential oil to each batch to start. (See the Safety Note for Grown-ups below.)

6. Store the dough in an airtight container or zip-top bag until it dries out. The dough should last up to 3 months if stored properly.

Here are some suggestions for color and scent combinations:

ALERTNESS: red or orange with orange essential oil

CONCENTRATION: green or yellow with lemongrass oil

CALMING: blue or purple with lavender oil

SAFETY NOTE FOR GROWN-UPS: Essential oils are very concentrated and should not be ingested. Not all oils are safe for children. Some children may be sensitive to some scents. Some oils that are safe for most kids include: lavender, lemon, lime, lemongrass, tea tree, bergamot, fir, grapefruit, clary sage, orange seed, frankincense, sandalwood, vetiver, and patchouli.

Walking a Labyrinth

"Labyrinth" is a fancy word for a special kind of maze that you can walk through. When you solve mazes on paper, you're trying to get from one end to the other. Walking through a labyrinth helps focus your mind and body on the same path by tracing a simple maze with your feet!

The easiest way to do this activity is outside with chalk. If you can't do it outside, you can make one inside with painter's tape. Or you can use a jump rope, strips of paper, ribbon, or a line of small toys to mark your path. The easiest shape to make is a simple spiral. Or you can create a more typical labyrinth. See the pictures below for examples of each.

What You'll Need

- Chalk, tape, small stones, or pieces of paper
- An open area of floor or ground

Directions

1. Draw or mark out a spiral path 6 to 10 feet across.

2. Start at the outside edge and slowly follow the path to the middle, then back out to the edge. Take as long as you need instead of trying to do it quickly.

3. If you want, count how many steps it takes to go from the beginning to the end of your labyrinth.

Create a Cozy Corner or Feelings Fort

When you're upset, what helps you calm down? Sometimes, it might be a hug or a sip of water. Other times, you may need some space and some quiet. It can really help to have a place to go when you're feeling overwhelmed. This can be a Cozy Corner or a Feelings Fort. Either way, this is a place for you to be safe and feel your feelings until they pass. A Cozy Corner is great if you have a corner available to make a little nook. A Feelings Fort may work better if you have limited space and prefer a darker tent-like area. There's no right or wrong way to set up your space. Choose what works for you.

What You'll Need

- The items that you circle in the "Things to Include" list below

Directions

1. Here's a list of questions to help you think of what to include. Circle yes or no for each question.

When you're upset, do you want anything
touching your body?   **YES   NO**

When you're upset, do you want to hold
something in your hands?   **YES   NO**

When you're upset, do you like noise or music?   **YES   NO**

When you're upset, do you like the lighting
to be dim/dark?   **YES   NO**

What helps you slow down your breathing?

What color helps you calm down?

What sounds help you relax?

2. Here are some ideas of things to include and ways they might help you. Circle any that you like. There are directions for how to make some of them in this book (see Mood Meter and Scented Squish Dough in chapter 1 and Glitter Jars in chapter 3). Choose what actually helps you. Your choices may be different from what a sibling or a friend would choose, and that's okay.

Things to Include:

- Soft blankets to snuggle under
- Pillows to hit or sit on
- A beanbag chair
- A soft chair or cushion
- A mat to lie on
- A tent so you don't have to look at too many things
- A way to play music
- A plant

- A stuffed animal to hug

- A Glitter Jar (page 88) or snow globe

- Beads or buttons to sort

- Fidget toys

- A water bottle to drink from

- A weighted blanket or toy

- Twinkle lights

- Sunglasses

- Gum

- Art supplies to draw your feelings or write a note

- A favorite book to read

- A scented rice bag

- Aromatherapy spray

- Scented Squish Dough (page 19)

- A print out of your Mood Meter (page 6)

COZY CORNER

FEELINGS FORT

Red Light Green Light

Red Light Green Light is a fun game where you get to move your body, listen carefully, and follow directions quickly. You can play inside or outside, but you might need to adjust if you're in a smaller space.

The point of the game is to cross from the starting line to the finish line as fast as possible, but the crossing guard controls the "traffic." When they say "red light," you have to stop, and when they say "green light," you have to start moving. If they catch you moving after saying "red light," you have to start over!

What You'll Need

- Masking tape or cones to mark the start and finish lines
- A few other kids

Directions

1. Mark the start and finish lines with the tape or cones.

2. Choose one person to be the crossing guard.

3. If you're outside, everyone can go as fast as they can. If you're inside, you may need to adjust and have people hop, crawl, or move in slow motion. Mix it up to have fun! (See Options on the next page.)

4. Decide if the first person to cross the line is the winner or if everyone has to cross the line to finish the game.

5. Everyone but the crossing guard should line up at the starting line.

6. The crossing guard should stand at the finish line, facing everybody else, and say, "green light."

7. Everyone starts to move toward the finish line.

8. When the crossing guard says, "red light," everyone has to freeze. If the crossing guard sees anyone move, that player has to go back to the starting line. (The crossing guard can add "yellow light" as an option where everyone has to move in slow motion.)

9. Depending on the rules you choose, each round of the game ends either when someone crosses the finish line or when the last person makes it across!

Options:

Here are some other ways to move from the starting to the finish line. You can use them just for older kids to even things out. Or everyone can use them just to mix things up.

- hop on one leg

- crab walk

- bear crawl

- run backward

- crawl on all fours

- roll seated on a scooter board (outside or on a smooth surface)

Goodnight Gratitude

Gratitude is a positive feeling that we often have but don't always take the time to talk about. When we're grateful, we notice and appreciate the good things in our lives. When you feel thankful (like after someone gives you a present or does something nice) or warm and happy, that's gratitude.

It can be easy not to notice how many wonderful things we have. If you have a place to live, your own bed or bedroom, food to eat, clean water, and friends and family, you have so much!

At the end of the day, it might be easier to think about what went wrong or what you didn't get. Maybe you're thinking about a toy you don't have or not getting your favorite meal for dinner. These things may make you feel upset or sad, but just like we can start our days with positive thoughts, we can end our days with gratitude.

It's important to practice gratitude because the more we do it, the better we get at it, just like playing an instrument or a sport. When you practice gratitude, you might notice that you start focusing more on good things that happen to you and appreciate the positive things in your life.

Directions

Before bed, simply list three things you're grateful for from the day. You can write them in a journal or say them out loud. Here are some examples:

> I'm grateful that we went to the park today.
>
> I'm grateful we had pizza for dinner.
>
> I'm grateful that I got to call my Grandma.

When you're just starting out, it can be easier to list things you can see or touch. After you've practiced gratitude for a while, try adding things that happened that made you happy.

> I'm grateful that I got to play with my best frend.
>
> I'm grateful Dad read me this morning.
>
> I'm grateful that I could listen to a podcast today.

Spray Away the Grumps and Gray

Everyone has days when they're in a gray and gloomy mood. Nothing seems to be going right, and everything seems hard. It's frustrating but normal. It's also not any fun.

Sometimes, when people try to cheer you up or tell you not to be grumpy, it can make you feel worse. But being in a bad mood is no fun. Your face gets tired of frowning. You might get a headache or a stomachache, and that can make you even grumpier!

But what can you do? Let's try sniffing our way out of it!

Sniffing? Yes, sniffing. You can mix up different sprays that can help boost your mood. Did you know your nose can tell apart hundreds of different smells? Here are a few ideas.

What You'll Need

- A small spray bottle (preferably glass)

- 3 ounces (6 tablespoons) water

- 1 ounce (2 tablespoons) witch hazel

- 5 to 10 drops of essential oils (See the Safety Note for Grown-Ups, page 33.)

- A grown-up to help with the essential oils

The essential oils each have a different smell. Here are some combinations you might like:

Cheer-up Spray:

If you're stuck in the grumps, a cheering spray may be what you need! The bright citrus smell will lift your spirits. To make this, combine these essential oils:

- Orange

- Grapefruit

- Geranium

Monster Spray:

Maybe you're in a mad monster mood. Use Monster Spray to help you reset yourself. To make this, combine these essential oils:

- Lavender

- Lemon

- Chamomile

Sweet Dreams Spray:

Try this mixture to help you relax and rest at bedtime. You can spray it in your room before you go to bed or spritz a little on your pillow to help you fall asleep.

- Lavender

- Vetiver

Directions

Mix all the ingredients together in the spray bottle.

SAFETY NOTE FOR GROWN-UPS: There are a lot of essential oils out there, so make sure to choose oils that are safe for kids (especially if you have younger children in your home). Be creative or use some of these ideas to get you started. Essential oils are very concentrated and should not be ingested. Not all oils are safe for children. Some children may be sensitive to some scents. The following oils are safe for most kids: lavender, lemon, lime, lemongrass, tea tree, bergamot, fir, grapefruit, clary sage, orange seed, frankincense, sandalwood, vetiver, and patchouli.

The Melting Ice Cube

Do you ever lie down at bedtime, but your brain is so full of thoughts that you can't even close your eyes? It can be hard to relax your body when your mind is racing. Maybe you're remembering all the fun you had earlier. Or you're so excited about tomorrow that it's hard to stop thinking about it. You can do this activity at any time of day, but it's great at bedtime to help you sleep. You can also practice for 5 to 10 minutes at other times of the day if you have some quiet time.

Directions

1. Lie down, preferably on your back, and make sure you're comfortable. Wiggle a little to settle in.

2. Picture an ice cube sitting on a table or sidewalk and melting into a puddle. That's going to be you!

3. If you're REALLY awake or wiggly, squeeze ALL the muscles in your body as hard as you can, count to five, and let them relax.

4. Take a long, slow breath in through your nose, and breathe out through your mouth. Do it three times.

5. Breathe in again, and this time, when you breathe out, relax so much that you feel like you're melting into your bed. Let the muscles in your legs, face, and stomach feel soft.

6. Breathe in again, and when you breathe out, relax your toes, your hands, and your neck.

7. Breathe in one more time, and when you breathe out this time, imagine that your kneecaps, shoulders, and forehead are getting soft.

8. Keep breathing in and "melting" as you breathe out for long as you need.

9. This kind of breathing is called deep breathing. If it's hard for you, try blowing all the air out of your lungs when you breathe out before you breathe in again. Or instead, just try to take very slow breaths if that's easier.

10. It's normal to think about things when you relax, but let any busy thoughts just melt away like an ice cube on a hot day.

Circle of Control

It's hard to be a kid sometimes! Grown-ups make a lot of decisions for you, and it can be frustrating to feel like you don't get any choices in your life.

But you probably have more control than you think! If you treat people with kindness, and they don't treat you that way, you can decide not to spend time with people like that. When you learn what you can control, you can worry less about what you can't control.

You also can't control your feelings, but you can choose how to show them. When you're upset, you can choose to hit a pillow to let those feelings out rather than hitting another person. Which sounds like a better choice to you?

The things you CAN control are:

- Your words
- Your actions
- Your behavior
- How you treat others
- How you handle your feelings
- What you learn
- How to spend your time
- Whether you forgive others
- What you wear
- Your friends

The things you CAN'T control are:

- Other people's words
- Other people's behavior
- How other people treat you
- Other people's feelings
- How tall you are
- The weather
- Time
- Whether other people like you

Directions

1. Inside the circle, write some things you can control, such as what you eat for breakfast, if you share a toy with your sibling, or if you clean your room.

2. Outside the circle, write things in your life that you can't control. For example, when the sun sets, if someone says something you don't like, if it rains, or what day the zoo is closed.

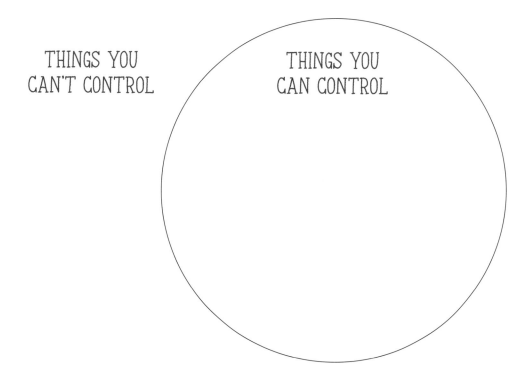

THINGS YOU
CAN'T CONTROL

THINGS YOU
CAN CONTROL

Cheetah, Chicken, Snail

When you're running really fast, it's hard to stop. It's called "momentum"! You need to slow your body down first. Sometimes, the same thing happens when we're excited, and we need to calm down. This activity can help you slow down gradually.

It's always fun to play, but games likes this can also be helpful. This activity can really help when you get home from a birthday party or from traveling someplace new, or when you've just had a really exciting day. It can help get those wiggles out before you need to sit down for a meal or start getting ready for bed.

What You'll Need

- Your active body

- An open space to run

- A "crash pad" (optional)

Directions

1. Run like a cheetah! Cheetahs are one of the fastest animals on earth, so zip around as fast as you can.

2. Now run around like a chicken. Do they walk in straight lines, or do they stop and change directions? Make your arms into wings and strut your stuff!

3. Last, get down on the ground and squirm like a snail. Snails don't move very fast. How long does it take you to move across the floor?

4. Now choose your own animal to imitate. Pick something fast, something really slow, and something in the middle. It could be "a rabbit, turtle, and caterpillar," or "a falcon, puppy, and sloth," or something else entirely. Experiment with your favorites.

Hopefully, by the time you're done, your body will feel more calm and ready to sit still or rest.

Make a Mandala

A Mandala is a circle with a special purpose. Drawing and looking at them can help you focus and relax. They come from the Hindu and Buddhist religions and represent the universe. Mandalas look complicated, but if you look closely, they actually repeat the same simple shapes over and over.

In this activity, you'll get to draw your own Mandala. You might need help from a grown-up to get started. The picture may turn out beautiful, but the most important part is actually the process of drawing it. How does your body feel during and after making a Mandala?

What You'll Need

- A bowl or plate
- Paper
- A pencil
- A pen or thin marker
- Colored pencils or markers

Directions

1. Trace the outside of a bowl or plate onto a piece of paper. You now have a circle to work with!

2. Next, draw an X and three circles inside the big circle. (See the first example on the next page.)

3. Now, starting at the center of the big circle, draw repeating shapes with a pen or thin marker. Then, move to the next circle, drawing whatever repeating shapes you'd like. (See the second example on the next page.)

4. When you fill the whole circle, you can stop, or you can go back and color in your Mandala.

5. Hang up your Mandala where you can see it and focus on its beauty.

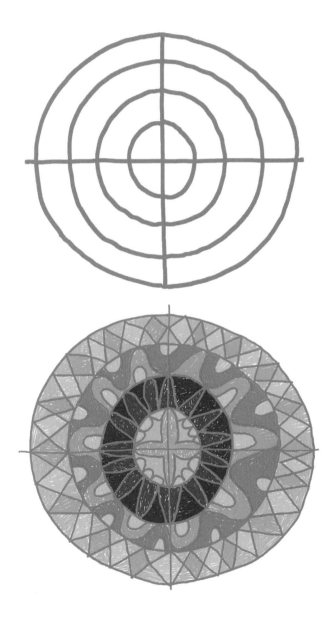

How Big Are Your Senses?

We use our five senses—sight, sound, smell, touch, and taste—to take in information about the world around us. But we all like different amounts of that information at a time.

Think of a time that something was too loud for you and you covered your ears, like at a fireworks display. Maybe someone else was okay with a noise that loud, but it hurt your ears. Or maybe someone at your house loves spicy food, but it's too big or strong tasting for you.

In this activity, you'll learn more about what you like and what you don't.

What You'll Need

- A pencil

Directions

Go through the following list and circle the answer that best describes how you feel.

1. In your school classroom or at your home, the amount of noise is: **okay / a lot / too much**

2. The lighting in your classroom or at home is: **okay / a lot / too much**

3. The chairs or seating arrangement in your classroom or home are: **okay / kind of uncomfortable / really uncomfortable**

4. The smells in your classroom or home are:
okay / a lot / too much

5. The length of time you have to sit at school or home is:
okay / a lot / too much

Go through the following list and circle how big or loud you like all of the things around you.

1. How much noise do you prefer? **A little / some / a lot**

2. How much light do you prefer? **A little / some / a lot**

3. How much do you like to be able to smell things?
A little / some / a lot

4. How soft of a seat do you prefer to sit on?
A little / some / a lot

5. How long can you sit in one place? **A little / some / a lot**

What do you need to change to make things work for you? For example, changing how bright the lights are or how close you are sitting to other people can make a big difference.

It can be hard to focus or stay calm when your classroom or home is too much for your body.

CHAPTER 2

Getting Along

In chapter 1, we focused on daily activities that can help us name and understand our feelings, learn how to stay calm, and move around in helpful ways. In this chapter, we'll talk about what happens when there are more people around—brothers and sisters, friends, kids at school, or even just people out in the world. It can be harder to deal with our own feelings when we have to think about other people's feelings, too. Many kids (and adults) might also feel nervous about new situations or people.

In this chapter, we'll talk about how to cooperate with your family, what you give to the world, how to look for chances to be kind, and how to manage when you disagree or don't want to share. Hopefully, these ideas will help you be a better friend and family member to the people you care about.

What Are Your Superpowers?

Wouldn't it be easier if we were all great at everything the first time we did it? We could do things easily without feeling frustrated, and we'd never lose at anything!

Unfortunately, that isn't how life works. Being frustrated, especially when learning new and challenging things, is part of life. However, we're all better at some things than at other things, and we're all good at different things. That's what makes everyone unique and interesting! It would be pretty boring if we were all exactly alike.

If you think about your favorite superheroes, they don't all have the same abilities. Some are super strong, some can fly, some can be invisible. Regular people have different strengths, too.

What You'll Need

- A pen or pencil

Directions

1. What if you thought of your strengths as superpowers? What are you good at? What do you love to do? Here are some examples:

   I am great at reading.

   I'm super helpful when I sweep and vacuum.

   I love animals and take good care of my pets.

In the space below, write down three of your superpowers.

My superpowers are:

_____

_____

_____

2. Now think about your friends' or family members' superpowers. Are they different from yours? Here are some examples:

   My sister loves math.

   My cousin is a fast runner.

   My friend always shares their toys with me.

In the space below, list some superpowers that your friends and family members have.

My friends' and family members' superpowers are:

_____

_____

_____

Family Joy Jar

All family members need to help out at home. This is true whether your family is just you and one grown-up, or if you have many siblings and other family members living with you. When things seem unfair, it can be easy not to notice the work that other people do for your family.

But living with people we love means we have to find ways to cooperate and get along. A Joy Jar can help everyone to notice the positive actions and contributions of other family members and to celebrate them together.

What You'll Need

- Craft pom-poms or felt balls

- A 1-quart jar or similar clear container

- A label for your jar (optional)

Directions

1. Put a few pom-poms at the bottom of the jar.

2. Place the jar in a part of your home where everyone can see and reach it.

3. Anytime someone does something that adds joy to the family or home, add a pom-pom to the jar. This could be all the kids playing cooperatively, taking turns without help, or cleaning up without a reminder.

4. Optional: If anyone (grown-ups included!) hurts some-one's feelings, you can take a pom-pom out. Decide as a family if you want to include this option.

5. When the Joy Jar is full, you can choose a family reward or adventure. Maybe it's a beach day, an ice cream outing, or a movie night. Ask a grown-up first.

6. Instead of using pom-poms, you can write down each kind action on a small piece of paper and put it in the jar. Then, when the jar is full, you can read them all to remind everyone of how much love you all have for each other.

Be an A-Maze-ing Friend

For this activity, pretend you and your friend are trying to go to the park, but they use a wheelchair and you need to find a path that doesn't have anything blocking their way. Your usual route is under construction.

What You'll Need

- A pen or pencil

Directions

In the maze below, try to find a way to get to the park that isn't blocked by construction.

Super Kindness Kid

Grab your cape, it's time to transform into SUPER KINDNESS KID! Today, we're going to think of ways to be SUPER KIND and make others SUPER HAPPY.

What You'll Need

- A pencil or pen
- A spiral notebook

Directions

1. First, we need to figure out your SUPERPOWERS to use for the forces of KINDNESS. Here are some examples to get you started. What else can you think of?

SUPERPOWER	HOW YOU CAN USE IT
Eagle Eyes	Help someone find something they lost
Super Strength	Help carry in the groceries
Ninja Noticing	Notice when someone is sad so you can try to cheer them up
Love Ray	Blast someone with your love power so they feel happy

2. Here are some sample missions. Choose one a day or have a kindness marathon.

   - Draw a picture to cheer someone up.

   - Write a note to mail to a friend or family member.

   - If you have your own money, use it to buy something your sibling or a grown-up really likes to give to them as a surprise.

   - Volunteer to do laundry or clean the house.

   - Make a video to send to a friend or family member telling them how much you love them.

   - Take food to a neighbor, friend, or community member in need.

3. What else could Super Kindness Kid do? Make a list of other ideas and how to use them.

YOUR SUPERPOWER	HOW YOU USE IT

4. Turn your spiral notebook into a Kindness Log. Write down (or ask a grown-up to write for you) each time you use one of your superpowers in your log.

Make a Magic Wand

If you've ever wished for a magic wand to solve your problems, now is your chance! The only hard part is that you have to make your own magic. It's easier than you think, though, when you use the magic of kindness and love.

First, you'll need to make a wand. Find a stick you can use as a nature wand; if there aren't any sticks nearby, there's another option. (See Alternative materials below.) Then, you'll need to create your spell book! Make sure you're using your powers for good.

What You'll Need

- A stick, 9 to 12 inches long

- A spool of 1-inch ribbon

- Hot glue and glue gun (get a grown-up to help with this part)

Alternative materials:

- Crayons, colored pencils, or markers

- White paper

- A pipe cleaner

- Tape

Directions

To create your wand:

1. Carefully glue the end of the ribbon to the tip of the stick.

2. Let the glue set, then wrap the ribbon around the stick.

3. When you get to the bottom of the stick, glue the ribbon again.

4. Leave extra ribbon below the place where you've glued it to the stick to create a ribbon tail, or add more ribbon for a dramatic effect.

Alternative:

1. Decorate a piece of white paper with whatever colors you like.

2. Place the middle of the pipe cleaner across one corner of the paper and roll the paper up to make a long, thin cone.

3. Tape the ends of the paper in place, and voilà, you have a wand!

To create your spells:

1. First, choose what magic you want to do and give it a name. Do you want to grant wishes? Help people get along? Give food to hungry people?

2. Next, decide what shape your spell will be. This will be the shape you trace in the air to cast your spell. There is one idea below, or you can draw your own.

3. Now cast your spells and make the world a better place!

MAGIC SPELL	WHAT IT DOES	SPELL SHAPE
Love Lightning	Makes person feel loved	[heart outline with a zigzag through it]

Guess How I Feel Game

In other activities, we've talked about how to know how you feel—what different feelings you have, how your body feels, what color your feelings are, and more. But how do other people know how YOU feel, and how do you know how OTHER PEOPLE feel?

The answer is something called body language, and it's actually more important than the words that we say. Body language is the way people's faces look when they are feeling different emotions. It's also how the rest of their bodies look. For example, someone might look down at the floor if they're feeling sad. If you understand body language, you can often figure out how they're feeling.

What You'll Need

- A mirror

- A pen or pencil

Directions

Now we're going to draw some of the ways people's faces look when they have different feelings. But first, look at your own face in the mirror and notice how each feeling looks.

1. Make a happy face.

   What is your mouth doing?

   How do your eyes look?

   What are your eyebrows doing?

2. Now draw a happy face.

3. Make a sad face.

What is your mouth doing?

How do your eyes look?

What are your eyebrows doing?

4. Now draw a sad face.

5. Make an angry face.

What is your mouth doing?

How do your eyes look?

What are your eyebrows doing?

6. Now draw an angry face.

7. Make a surprised face.

What is your mouth doing?

How do your eyes look?

What are your eyebrows doing?

8. Now draw a surprised face.

9. Make a scared face.

What is your mouth doing?

How do your eyes look?

What are your eyebrows doing?

10. Now draw a scared face.

11. Make an excited face.

   What is your mouth doing?

   How do your eyes look?

   What are your eyebrows doing?

12. Now draw an excited face.

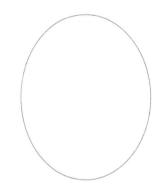

13. Now make each face and see if someone else can guess what you're feeling.

Apology Fill-in-the-Blanks

Everyone makes mistakes or says or does something they feel sorry about. Sometimes, we feel so bad about what happened that it's hard to even look at or talk to the person we've hurt.

A lot of grown-ups never learned how to apologize, which is why it's important to start practicing now! We might think that saying we're sorry makes it sound like we're bad people for messing up or hurting someone, but apologizing just means that you care about that person.

But when you feel terrible, it can be tough to think of what to say. When we get embarrassed or upset and start blaming other people for a mistake we've made, it's called being defensive. When we admit we made a mistake—even when it's hard—it's called taking responsibility.

Here are some examples of both:

- "I'm sorry I stepped on your foot, but you were in my way."

Is this taking responsibility or being defensive?

- "I'm sorry if you were upset, but you made me mad."

Is this taking responsibility or being defensive?

- "I'm sorry I knocked down your tower. It was an accident, but I should have looked where I was going. Can I help you rebuild it?"

Is this taking responsibility or being defensive?

- "I'm sorry I hurt your feelings when I said that. I was upset, but it's not okay to call you a name. Can I give you a hug?"

Is this taking responsibility or being defensive?

Even if it wasn't on purpose, we can admit that we made a mistake. For example, offering to rebuild the tower is called making amends, and it is a way to repair the harm done.

You are allowed to have feelings, but it's not okay to hurt people. When we do, we need to apologize.

What You'll Need

- A pencil or pen

Directions

Now you try. Fill in the blanks with a mistake you've made and what you can do to make amends.

I'm sorry I _____. I should have

_____. Next time,

I will _____.

Can I _____?

Send Your Sibling to Space!

Having siblings (brothers and sisters) is HARD! Sometimes, you're best friends. It's great to always have someone to play with at home. You can team up against your grown-ups!

But you also have to share your grown-ups with them. Sometimes, you want to play different things. Or you might have different interests. And sometimes, they're just plain annoying.

It doesn't matter if you're the oldest, the youngest, or in the middle. When what you want and what your siblings want is different, it can be very hard.

And you can't just leave, like you do when you and a friend are having a hard time together. You and your sibling probably live at the same place!

But what if you could at least pretend to escape for a while? Or get rid of that pesky sibling for a bit? If you have a little time to snuggle with a grown-up, you can play this game out loud. Or if you feel like drawing, you can even make a mini book!

(If you don't have siblings, these problems can still come up with friends you see a lot.)

What You'll Need

- A grown-up to talk to (NOT your sibling!)
- Paper and colored pencils or markers

Directions

1. Make sure your sibling is not nearby or even at home. This is a great activity to do during special time with a grown-up. It's not meant to hurt your sibling's feelings, no matter how upset you are; it's to help you work out your feelings about the situation.

2. Make a list of things you don't like about having siblings, no matter how small. Either write them down, draw them, or say them out loud. Maybe it feels like they always get their way, they have more toys than you, they get more treats, or they get to do everything they want.

3. Think of a way to get rid of them. Then, write it down, draw it, or say it out loud. Will you sell them at a yard sale? Return them to the store? Ship them to another country in a box? Send them into space on a rocket ship? Get creative!

4. Keep writing, drawing, or saying your ideas until you run out—or until you start to feel you might miss them if you really got rid of them. Remember that it's okay to have big feelings. It's better to get those feelings out than to pretend they don't exist and try to hold them inside until you get angry.

5. Remember, you don't actually get to send your sibling to space unless they become an astronaut when they grow up. But it's fun to pretend, isn't it?

Social Story Comics

Do you ever feel nervous when you go somewhere new? Maybe you feel butterflies in your tummy or it's hard to sit still. Everyone feels anxious sometimes, even grown-ups. It often happens when we have to do something we've never done before because we don't know what to expect.

One way we can feel calmer about going to a new place is by knowing as much as we can about what to expect ahead of time.

We can do this by making a Social Story. It's like a mini comic book about a situation.

What You'll Need

- A grown-up to help you with the steps
- Paper
- A pen or pencil

Directions

1. Think of a new situation you're worried about.

2. Think about all of the steps involved in this situation. For example, in the illustration below, someone is going to a restaurant they've never been to before. Look at the steps they think they'll be taking.

3. Fold your paper into a book or make rectangles for a comic strip.

4. Have your grown-up help you draw and write the steps you'll probably take in your new situation.

5. Read your book until you feel more comfortable about your new situation.

Going to a New Restaurant

We drive to the restaurant.

We wait to be shown to a table.

We read the menu and order food.

We wait until the server brings our food.

Refill Your Snuggle Cup

It's hard being a kid. It feels like you never get to do what you want. Grown-ups make a lot of choices for you, and they're always so busy! When you want to tell them things, sometimes they don't pay attention, or they're in a hurry, or they're trying to get you to go somewhere. When it feels like someone isn't really listening to us, it doesn't feel very good.

Also, if grown-ups are away at work for a long time, you might miss them a lot and need to spend some time with them when they get home. I call this special time refilling your Snuggle Cup.

What You'll Need

- Yourself

- Someone you love

Directions

Things to think about before you refill your Snuggle Cup:

1. How big is your Snuggle Cup? Some people have a small Snuggle Cup that just needs a quick hug to refill it. Some people have a Snuggle Cup as big as a mountain!

2. How full is your Snuggle Cup? Is it totally empty or just half empty? Do you need one snuggle to refill it or twenty?

Things to do before you refill your Snuggle Cup:

3. Choose a snuggle spot. It could be a couch, chair, bed, or the floor.

4. Name your snuggle! Do you need a tight hug or a light squeeze? A hug and kiss or an arm around your shoulders? Tell your grown-up.

5. Figure out how many snuggles you need? Pick a number between one and a million. (You can count by 100,000s to get there.)

When you're ready to refill your Snuggle Cup:

6. Let your grown-up know it's time, and then SNUGGLE! And make sure your Snuggle Cup feels full. Do you feel better?

How Does Your Anger Feel?

Can you think of a time you were ANGRY? Why did it happen? What does it feel like in your body?

It's important to know that it's okay and normal to be angry. Things happen that are upsetting. When we're angry, it can be hard to control our bodies, though, and no matter how we feel, it's NOT OKAY to hurt people. Sometimes, we get the message that anger is bad. That's not true. No feelings are good or bad, they're just a temporary way that our bodies react.

So, how does your body feel when you're angry? Does your face feel hot? What are your eyebrows doing? Does your chest feel tight? Are your hands relaxed and open or clenched shut? Are your shoulders up or down? What else do you notice?

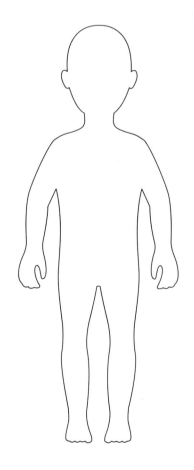

What You'll Need

- A pen or pencil
- A piece of paper

Directions

1. On the following outline, write down how each part of your body feels when you're mad.

Head:

Face:

Chest:

Shoulders:

Arms:

Hands:

Tummy:

Legs:

Feet:

2. Often, when we're angry, the anger is actually covering up another strong feeling. But that other feeling is so strong that we're trying to avoid it, so we get angry instead.

Can you think of the last time you were mad? What was it about? Can you think about what you might have been feeling underneath? Write down the strong feeling you think you might have been covering up and what it was about.

Here are some examples of feelings that are so strong you might cover them up and feel angry instead:

- Sadness because someone is leaving for work or a friend is moving away

- Fear of someone getting sick

- Worry about being hungry

- Frustration because someone compared you to a sibling or another child

- Disappointment because your parent changed a planned trip to the zoo

- Embarrassment about a mistake you made in front of your friends

- Jealousy because a friend has something you really want

- Hurt because you feel like a sibling or classmate is the favorite

Make a Human Burrito

Think of a time you just needed a really big hug. Being wrapped up and squeezed is called deep pressure, and it can help our bodies and brains calm down and feel safe.

If your body is feeling wiggly or buzzy or your mind just can't slow down, there are other ways than hugs to get that deep pressure. You can do this alone or recruit a "burrito maker"—a grown-up, sibling, or friend—to help.

What You'll Need

- A blanket that's bigger than you (not a baby blanket)
- A helper (optional)

Directions

1. Lay the blanket out on the floor.

2. Choose some imaginary fillings for your burrito, like rice and beans and cheese.

3. If you have a helper, have them fill the burrito with you and your chosen imaginary fillings. Have them squish some rice and beans on you, sprinkle cheese on top, or *thwap* a delicious blob of guacamole on you.

4. Move over so the edge of the blanket is at your neck and your head stays clear. Then roll yourself up in the blanket (or have your helper do it) until you're a nice snug burrito.

5. If you have a big enough helper, they can carefully pull you across the floor by your feet if you want them to.

Animal Walk Dice Game

When you need to get your wiggles out, this is a fun way to do it. You can play this game any time, but it's especially helpful if the weather is keeping you inside. That's because all you need is your body and a little space.

You can play by yourself, but if another person is around, you can play together. You can take turns or do these walks at the same time.

What You'll Need

- A six-sided die

- Enough space to move around

Directions

1. Roll the die to see what number you get.

2. Now look at the list of Animal Walks and move around like the animal that matches the number you rolled.

3. If you have more than one player, take turns rolling the die.

Animal Walks:

1. **Bear Walk:** Bend at the waist and walk on your hands and feet like a bear, with your legs mostly straight. Keep your hips lifted.

2. **Crab Scuttle:** Sit on the ground, lean back, put your hands slightly behind you, then lift your bottom to walk on your hands and feet. Try moving sideways like a real crab.

3. **Kangaroo Hops:** Tuck your elbows by your sides and hop with your feet together like a kangaroo.

4. **Frog Jumps:** Squat on the floor and jump like a frog. You can play leapfrog with another player.

5. **Inchworm Crawl:** Bend over with straight legs and place your hands on the ground, walk your hands forward until your body is mostly straight, then walk your feet up to your hands. Repeat.

6. **Duck Waddles:** Tuck your hands under your arms like wings, squat, and waddle like a duck.

The Fancy Restaurant Game

Some parts of eating at a restaurant are really fun: getting to pick your own food, choosing dishes you might not eat at home, and seeing what interesting things the restaurant has to keep you occupied.

But some parts are a little boring. You might have to wait for a table, then it feels like your food takes forever to arrive, and you have to sit without running around. If you don't go to restaurants very often, it can be easy to forget what it's like.

Pretending to be at a very fancy restaurant at home can help you remember the rules of eating out while being a little silly. Be creative!

What You'll Need

- At least one other diner
- A table with chairs
- Menus (real or pretend)
- Dishes and napkins
- A notepad and pen
- A timer (optional)

Directions

1. Choose who will be the server and who will be the diner at your very, very fancy restaurant.

2. The server welcomes the diner to the restaurant and escorts them to their table. The server might have a fancy accent or special uniform.

3. Once the diner is seated, the server presents the menu. You can make your own menu or just pretend. Do you have daily specials? Anything your diner should know?

4. The diner chooses their meal and orders it from the server. The server can write this down on their notepad.

5. Now the server goes to get the food and the diner has to wait! You can time how long it takes if you want.

6. The server comes back with the (pretend) food, and the diner gets to enjoy it. When the diner's done, the server takes the dishes back. Make sure the diner pays for their meal before they leave!

Feeling Faces Card Game

When you feel sad or angry, do you say that out loud to people? Probably not. So, how do we know how other people feel if they don't tell us? Well, they actually do, but not in words.

As we learned in the Guess How I Feel Game (page 57), when someone's face or body shows their feelings, it's called body language. But it can be tricky to understand a person's body language if we're not paying attention.

This game can help you connect people's feelings to their body language. It can be played by two or more players.

What You'll Need

- Index cards, card stock, or heavy paper cut into squares or rectangles

- A pen or pencil

Directions

To make the cards:

1. Take two blank squares or rectangles. On one, write the name of a feeling. On the other, draw a face showing that feeling. Look at the List of Feelings on the next page for ideas, or come up with your own.

To play:

2. If you're by yourself, lay out all the cards facedown. Choose two cards and try to match the face to the feeling.

3. If you have someone else to play with:

   ◆ Take turns drawing a card.

   ◆ If you choose a card with a face, make that face and ask the other person to guess what feeling it is.

   ◆ If you choose a card with a word, make up a short story where you might feel that way and have the other player guess the feeling. For example, if you choose a card with the word "sad," your story might be about losing your favorite toy.

List of Feelings

Sad

Angry

Happy

Excited

Proud

Scared

Nervous

Joyful

Surprised

Worried

Loving

Embarrassed

My Friends' Favorite Things

You know what all of your favorite things are, but what do your favorite people like? Sometimes, it's easy to think of a gift we might want or a food we like to eat, but that doesn't mean someone else will like it, too. It might be hard to imagine that your friend, sibling, or relative doesn't like bananas or graphic novels or your favorite movie! But they might not.

What You'll Need

- A pen or pencil

Directions

1. Think of three of your favorite people and try to put your-self in their shoes (that means imagine what it's like to be them). How much do you know about what they like?

2. Now, fill in the blanks below with what you THINK they like. Then, ask, call, or have a grown-up help you text or email them to ask what their answers actually are. Were you surprised?

QUESTION	YOUR ANSWER	THEIR ANSWER	DO THEY MATCH?
Favorite Color			
Favorite Food			
Favorite Animal			
Favorite Movie			
What Makes Them Happy?			
What Makes Them Proud?			

When we try to imagine how another person feels, it's called empathy. It's okay to like different things than our friends and families. We don't have to make negative comments about things they like and we don't, and having empathy helps us be better friends.

So, if you guessed a lot of their favorite things wrong, that doesn't mean you're a bad friend! And since you asked them for the right answer, now you know. When it's their birthday or they need something to cheer them up, you'll have a good idea of what might help.

"How Can I Help?" Picture Search

In a lot of books or TV shows, someone starts yelling, "Help! Help!" The heroes know that someone needs a hand, and they run over to save them. In real life, it's not always that obvious when somebody needs help. You might say something like, "I can't reach that," instead of, "Please help me get that down." Can you tell the difference between those two phrases?

How do we know when someone is having a hard time and could use some help? We have to be observant. That means noticing what's happening around us and how people act. You might have practiced this in other activities in this book by figuring out how people feel based on their facial expressions. In books and movies, people who need help are often in immediate danger, too. In daily life, that's not as common. You may not need to swoop in and save someone's life, but you can still lend a helping hand and improve someone's day.

Directions

Look at the picture and find 6 people who need help. Where are they? What do they need? What could you do to help?

Secret Sign Language

How would you like to be able to talk to your siblings or friends without anyone hearing you? You could make secret plans. You could discuss fun surprises. You could talk across the room without being overheard!

There are actually people who do this all the time. They use their hands to talk in a language called American Sign Language (ASL). Who are they? They're people who can't hear well or who are deaf. Some deaf people can hear a little bit; others can't hear at all.

With ASL, names and some other words are spelled out by people with their hands. It's called finger spelling, and you can use it to send secret messages to others.

Directions

1. Here is the alphabet using finger spelling. Can you figure out how to sign your name?

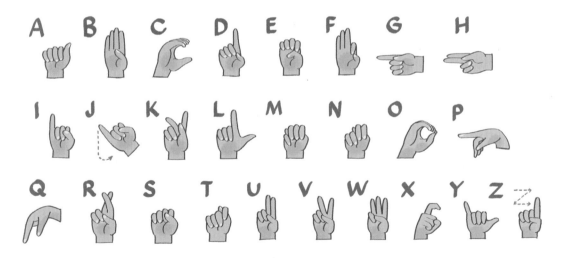

2. If you want to learn more, ask a grown-up to help you find videos or books about ASL. It uses unique movements to mean whole words and phrases. Here's how to sign "I love you."

3. What else can you spell with your hands?

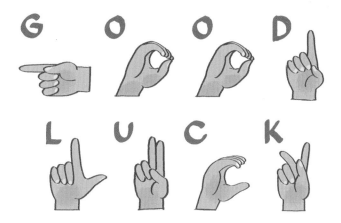

Big Feelings

Being a kid can be great when you get to play and have fun. You might not have to go to work or pay bills, but you don't get to make all the decisions about how you spend your time, either. You might have to go to school or daycare, you don't get to pick all your clothes, and you don't get to eat what you want all the time. It can be frustrating to feel like you don't get to control your time or what's around you.

Some days, that's a little annoying; other days, it's just too much. When so many little things build up inside and explode, those are some BIG feelings. It can be scary when you have feelings like that! Grown-ups might even be upset or uncomfortable with your big feelings, which can make you feel bad.

But feelings aren't good or bad. They can be small or big, gentle or strong, quiet or loud, or soft or prickly. Feelings aren't forever. This chapter has ideas to help you avoid those big feelings explosions in the first place or practice calming down when they come up. This chapter will also help you manage what you do when you're upset, ask for what you need, and get those feelings out of your body.

Glitter Jars

Making Glitter Jars is a fun craft project and gives you a great relaxation tool at the end! You can make one at a time or a whole batch with a group of friends. This is a useful item to have in a Cozy Corner or Feelings Fort (page 23) for when you're upset. Glitter Jars are great when you want to look at something calming and interesting.

What You'll Need

- A grown-up to help you
- An empty clear bottle (water bottle or bottle available in craft stores for $1 to $3)
- A bowl with a pour spout or a small funnel
- Hot water
- Clear glue or corn syrup
- Food coloring
- Glitter (See Note to Grown-Ups about Glitter.)
- Beads, sequins, hot glue, or super glue (optional)

NOTE TO GROWN-UPS ABOUT GLITTER: Different colors and sizes will give you different effects. Fine glitter will swirl more and stay suspended longer. Having mixed sizes in one bottle gives a variety of speeds. Adding beads or sequins also adds interest.

Directions

1. Have a grown-up whisk together the hot water and the glue or corn syrup. The amount will depend on the size and number of your bottles, but use about 20 percent glue and 80 percent water, or 50 percent corn syrup and 50 percent water. The thicker the liquid, the slower the swirling will be.

2. Use the pour spout or funnel to help fill the bottle with your liquid mixture.

3. Add a few drops of food coloring, and ¼ to ½ teaspoon of glitter. Try some of the combinations listed on the next page, or get creative!

4. Add the beads or sequins (if using).

5. Put the lid on the bottle and swirl together. Flip the bottle over to test it out. Add more food coloring or glitter if needed.

6. Use hot glue or super glue to attach the lid more permanently. Let the glue dry before using it again.

7. Turn your bottle over and watch the glitter swirl and settle. Repeat!

Some fun combinations:

NAME	FOOD COLORING	GLITTER COLOR
Ocean	Blue and green	Silver and blue
Galaxy	Black	Purple and blue
Beach	Blue and green	Gold and silver
Halloween	Orange	Black and silver
Slime	Green and yellow	Green and gold
Lava	Red and yellow	Red, orange, and gold
Unicorn	Purple	Pink, purple, and silver

Shape Breathing

We've talked a lot about how our bodies feel when we're upset. When our feelings are really big, it can be harder to control our bodies. One way to calm down is by breathing. We can actually trick our brains into thinking we're calm by breathing through our noses.

The hard part is that we have to breathe slowly. That can be really tough when we're upset, so that's where shape breathing comes in. The shapes give you a guide to help you slow down, and tracing the shape lets your brain focus on something else.

Practice this activity when you're already calm so you know how it works, then you can give it a try when you need some help slowing down your breath.

What You'll Need

- One of the shapes in the picture below
- Your finger

Directions

1. Pick a shape and start at the dot. Follow the arrows with your finger.

2. Slowly trace the shape with your finger. Breathe in for four counts. Hold for four counts. Breathe out for four counts. Hold for four counts. Repeat.

3. Trace the shape four times and see how you feel. Keep tracing and breathing until you feel calmer.

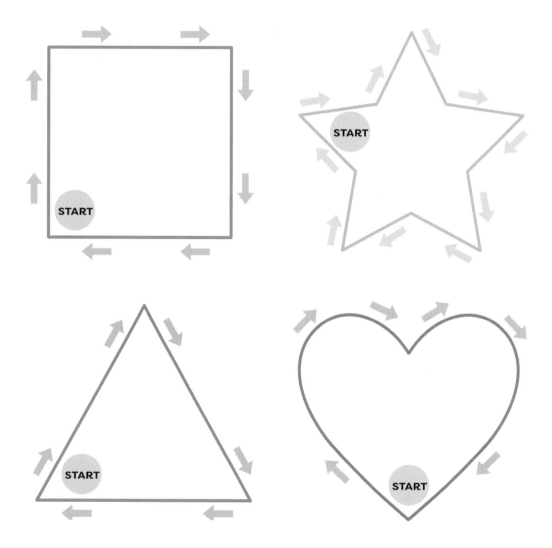

How Full Is Your Backpack?

Think of a day when everything seems to go wrong. It's not one big thing but a lot of smaller things until finally—BAM!—you can't take it anymore. Whether you cry or throw things or hit someone, you just need to get your feelings out RIGHT NOW.

This happens to everyone at some point, and some people call it unloading your emotional backpack. Each time something happens, and we don't feel safe expressing our feelings, we shove those feelings into an imaginary backpack. When that backpack is full, we can't fit any more emotions inside, and the zipper explodes! Now we have to unpack all those feelings stuffed in the backpack—and also fix the zipper.

In a perfect world, we wouldn't shove all those feelings into our backpacks, we would just let them out as they came up. But if you're worried that you'll get in trouble, or if someone is telling you to stop crying, it makes sense that you want to pretend you're okay. Sometimes, we save up all these feelings until we're with someone we know will love us no matter how big our feelings get. In this activity you'll think of examples that might fill up your backpack. Sometimes adults think that whatever happened right before you get upset it was caused it, but it might have been five little things that day.

What You'll Need

- A pen or pencil

Directions

1. Think of all the things that might happen in a day that would go into your emotional backpack.

2. Write them in the backpack below to see how it fills up with everything, and then overflows!

Here are some ideas:

- You fall and get hurt
- You drop your breakfast
- You can't find your shoes
- Someone calls you a name
- Someone wasn't listening to you

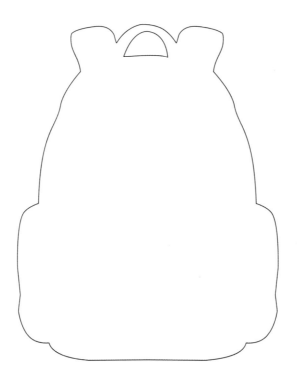

Where Do I Feel My Feelings?

Our feelings aren't just imaginary things we make up. They're reactions in our bodies, just like a sneeze or being thirsty. In the same way, they don't last forever. It's helpful to know what different feelings do to our bodies so we know how to identify and name them, and then calm down.

What You'll Need

- A pen or pencil

Directions

1. Think about each of the feelings listed below, and then place the number on the cartoon body where you feel them.

2. Next, write down how it feels. For example, when you're happy, you may feel warm and sparkly in your heart. Or, when you're frustrated, your throat may feel heavy and sticky. Anger might feel hot, red, and tingly. Maybe it has a color or a texture or a temperature. There are no wrong answers because they're YOUR feelings.

1. HAPPY

When I'm happy, my body feels _____ .

2. SAD

When I'm sad, my body feels _____ .

3. ANGRY

When I'm angry, my body feels _____ .

4. DISAPPOINTED

When I'm disappointed, my body feels _____ .

5. FRUSTRATED

When I'm frustrated, my body feels _____ .

6. JEALOUS

When I'm jealous, my body feels _____ .

7. EXCITED

When I'm excited, my body feels _____ .

8. NERVOUS

When I'm nervous, my body feels _____ .

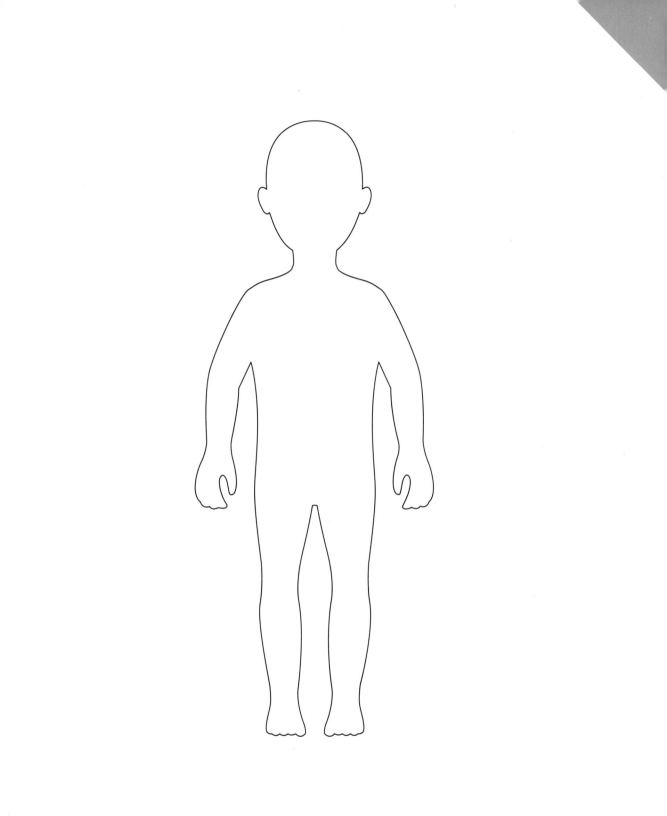

The Stress Monster Smash

Have you ever been so mad that you wanted to hit things? When our bodies are stressed, they go into what's called fight or flight mode. That fight part is what makes us want to hit or kick, and the flight part makes us want to run away. But we can't always run, especially if we're at home, and no matter how angry we get, it's not okay to hit people.

So, how can you get all that energy out of your body? Here's one way: smashing the stress monster.

What You'll Need

- Play-Doh, clay, or Scented Squish Dough (page 19)

Directions

1. Roll the dough into a ball.

2. You can leave it as a ball or shape it into a little monster. Does it have eyes? Arms? Tentacles?

3. Which feeling or thing you're mad about does it represent? Is it a worry monster? Your sibling for always wanting to take your stuff? Your grown-up's work schedule? A friend moving away?

4. Smash it! You can pound it into a pancake, tear it in half, or poke it with your finger. Get those feelings out in a safe way.

5. Make another stress monster and do it again!

How to Make a Pinwheel

Pinwheels are just plain fun, but they're also great for helping our bodies and brains slow down. There's something about blowing on a pinwheel, and then watching it spin that has a soothing effect. If you have trouble with the other breathing exercises in this book, the pinwheel might be easier.

What You'll Need

- Card stock or heavy-weight paper
- Scissors
- Hot glue gun and glue
- A grown-up to help with the glue gun
- A thumbtack
- A small bead
- A wooden skewer, dowel, or plastic/paper drinking straw

Directions

To make your pinwheel:

1. On a separate sheet of paper, draw a pinwheel using template below.

2. Cut along the lines and fold the tips in toward the center. Attach the tips with a small amount of hot glue.

3. Carefully push the thumbtack through the center. Place the bead on the tack, then push the tack into the skewer with a little room so it can spin. Let the glue set for a bit.

To use your pinwheel:

4. First, sit comfortably in a chair and try to relax your body.

5. Blow on the pinwheel using long, deep breaths. How does your body feel?

6. Now use short, quick puffs to spin the pinwheel. How does that feel?

7. Next, inhale deeply, hold for two seconds, and blow out slowly to see how long you can make the pinwheel spin.

8. How does each way of breathing make your body feel? Grab your pinwheel when you need help slowing down your body, or keep it in your Cozy Corner.

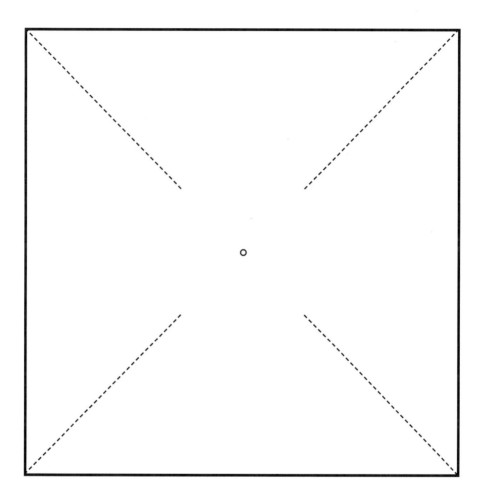

Calm-Down Box

Wouldn't it be great if you could take your Cozy Corner or Feelings Fort (page 23) around with you? In a way, you can. A Calm-Down Box is a small bin of objects that helps you relax. You can take it in the car, bring it with you on vacation, or put it in your Cozy Corner at home.

A Calm-Down Box is a great tool for when you're feeling worried or nervous or having a hard time slowing down your mind. The list below has lots of ideas, but choose items that you actually like. Some people like one smell or texture, but others don't.

What You'll Need

- A shoebox or plastic bin

- At least one item from each category listed on the next page

Directions

Fill your Calm-Down Box with items from the following list or come up with some of your own ideas.

THINGS THAT SMELL GOOD	BEAUTIFUL IMAGES	DELICIOUS FOODS	PEACEFUL SOUNDS OR MUSIC	SOOTHING TEXTURES
A bottle or vial of perfume	A postcard or photo of a favorite place	Something crunchy like nuts or pretzels	A music player with a calming playlist	A favorite stuffed animal
A small bottle of essential oils (lemon, lemongrass, orange, peppermint, and lavender are good options)	A piece of soothing art	Hard candies to suck on in a strong flavor you like	Noise-cancelling headphones	Therapy putty or kinetic sand
A cotton ball in a small bottle with a few drops of essential oil	A family photo	Chewy foods, like beef jerky or dried fruit	A white noise machine	Silk ribbon or fabric
A small pillow of dried herbs	A small piece of comforting jewelry	Gum	A drum or rain stick	A sensory toy

Shred Your Feelings

There are lots of reasons you might feel upset, be in a bad mood, or have big feelings. Even small things that might sound silly to someone else can really be upsetting. If you're having some thoughts or worries that keep coming up, this activity can help you get rid of them.

   Sometimes, it's hard to manage feelings because they're thoughts in our heads or sensations in our bodies. By writing them down, we can turn them into something we can see, touch, and destroy!

What You'll Need

- A grown-up

- Paper

- A pen or pencil

- A paper shredder, scissors, or fireplace (optional)

Directions

1. Write down (or have a grown-up help) or draw pictures of everything you can think of that's annoying, frustrating, unfair, scary, or anything else that makes you mad or upset. This could be a bully at school, bad weather, an itchy bug bite on your leg, a toy breaking, or your sibling being loud.

2. Now decide how you want destroy these worries. You can simply crumple up the paper and throw it in the trash, run it through a paper shredder with a grown-up's help, or use scissors to cut the paper into tiny pieces. If you have a fireplace, you can have a grown-up help you burn the paper.

Here are some prompts and ideas to get you started:

I'm too _____.

I wish I were more _____.

I'm worried that no one will want to play with me.

It's not fair that I never get to choose the movies at home.

I'm scared my grandparent will get sick.

I'm nervous about moving and traveling to a new place.

Dragon Breath

You've probably noticed a few different ways to help you breathe deeply in this book. It's a really useful skill for kids and adults alike! But not every version works for every person, which is why there are a lot of ways to do it. This is another fun activity that lets you use your imagination.

What You'll Need

- A comfy place to sit

Directions

1. Sit down in your comfy place and pretend you're a giant dragon sitting on your giant, shiny pile of treasure.

2. Take a big, deep breath in through your nose like you're trying to smell for any signs of humans (or dwarves) coming to steal your gold. You're trying to smell as far away as you can so no one can sneak up on you.

3. Now open your mouth wide and breathe out as big a blast of fire as you can! Make your breath go as far as you can so no one can approach the glittering mountain of gems and coins underneath you. How long can you breathe out that fire?

4. Smell for intruders again! Take a deep breath in through your nose for any scent of treasure hunters. Then exhale a huge stream of dragon fire just in case you missed something. Repeat one more time until you're a calm, relaxed dragon on your glittering golden treasure.

Visualize Your Happy Place

When you're having very big feelings, everything seems to make them worse. By using a technique called visualization, we can help our brains focus on something else so we can stop thinking about what's upsetting us. You're always allowed to be upset, but if you're having a hard time calming your body down, this is a way to help.

A visualization is like playing pretend or watching a movie inside your head. The more details you can add, the better, but it takes some practice. Don't worry if it's a little hard the first time you try.

What You'll Need

- A comfy place to sit or lie down
- A grown-up or somebody else who can read

Directions

1. Sit or lie down so you're comfortable and can relax.

2. Close your eyes and have someone read "The Island" (on the next page) to you.

3. As they read it, try to imagine all the details. Notice how your body feels.

4. After you've done this visualization a few times, you won't need anybody to read to you. Instead, you'll be able to imagine the island on your own!

THE ISLAND

Imagine you're walking near a large, calm lake. It's near sunset, and the water on the lake is very smooth. There's a gentle breeze blowing on your skin. You notice a small boat on the shore of the lake. You get in and sit down. The boat starts gliding quietly across the water. You notice how calm and clear the lake is, and you take a deep breath of cool air.

After a few minutes, you notice an island coming into view. The island is covered in green trees, and you hear birds chirping. The boat gently bumps to a stop on the shore, and you get out of the boat and stand on the island.

You notice a path into the trees and start walking that way. The path is clear and wide and shaded by the dense trees. You walk for a few minutes, listening to the rustling leaves, the chirping birds, and the sound of your own soft footsteps.

Then, you see the trees give way to an open area of soft grass next to a small stream. You go and sit or lie down in the soft grass, feeling the sunlight and breeze on your skin as you listen to the sound of the moving water. You breathe in the sweet air and exhale deeply. You are at peace.

Putting Out a Feelings Fire

Sometimes, our feelings can be like a fire: They can flare up quickly and burn strongly. But there are three ways to manage a fire. One is to add more fuel to keep it burning. Another is to let it burn out. The third is to try to put it out faster.

Here are some ideas for managing a Feelings Fire.

Things that add fuel to a Feelings Fire:

- Someone telling you your feelings are wrong, or that you shouldn't feel that way

- Being ignored or sent away

- Being told to stop feeling that way

Ways to let the Feelings Fire burn out:

- Using a breathing exercise until the flames die down

- Hitting a pillow until the feelings pass

- Drawing your feelings

How to put out the Feelings Fire faster:

- Having someone listen to your feelings and try to understand (empathy)

- Going to a Cozy Corner or Feelings Fort (page 23)

- Swinging or making yourself into a Human Burrito (page 73)

What You'll Need

- A pen or pencil

Directions

On the lines below, write about what happens when you're upset. What makes it worse? What helps you slow down? What helps get those feelings out?

Things that add to my Feelings Fire:

_____

_____

_____

Things that let my Feelings Fire burn out:

_____

_____

_____

Things that help put out my Feelings Fire faster:

_____

_____

_____

Create a Calm Down Menu

There are a lot of activities in this book! Whether you read it straight through or jumped around, I hope you found new tools and strategies that help you feel calmer and happier in your life. Even if you did, it can still be hard to think of them in the moment when you are upset.

That's why it can help to pick some of them ahead of time. Think of which activities helped the most or go find one you haven't tried if you're not sure. Then, you can fill in the following chart or make your own chart to hang up as a reminder. Next time you're having big feelings, you can look at it to remind yourself what was helpful.

What You'll Need

- A pen or pencil

Directions

1. Think of a time when you were sad. What helped cheer you up? It could be a hug, reading a favorite story with a grown-up or sibling, or wrapping up in a cozy blanket. Write it down on the chart.

2. When you were angry, what worked to help you get those feelings out? Was it a calming exercise? Smashing a Stress Monster (page 98) or a pillow? A visualization or drawing your feelings? An affirmation? Something else? Write it down on the chart.

3. When you were worried, how did you help your body relax? Being a Human Burrito (page 73)? Listening to music in your Cozy Corner or Feelings Fort (page 23)? Drawing a Mandala (page 40)? Write it down on the chart.

Try to list at least three things that help with each feeling. You can put the list in in your Cozy Corner, in your room, on the fridge, or wherever you'll see it when it's needed.

WHEN I'M SAD, IT HELPS TO …	WHEN I'M ANGRY, IT HELPS TO …	WHEN I'M WORRIED, IT HELPS TO …

RESOURCES

Dayna Abraham's website, Lemon Lime Adventures, is great for dealing with challenging behaviors for kids who are wired differently and neurodivergent: LemonLimeAdventures.com.

Playful Parenting by Dr. Lawrence Cohen is an incredible book for parents and caregivers that offers playful solutions to get to the root of your child's behavior.

eeBoo is a mother-run company with a selection of social and emotional intelligence and other games and toys. eeBoo.com/pages /developing-the-whole-child.

If you need sensory or fidget toys or chewable items, Fat Brain Toys has great options. (The simpl dimpl is a favorite here.) FatBrainToys.com.

If you need some ideas for Magic Morning Mantras (page 4) or just want them done for you, The Renegade Mama has an affirmation deck for kids: TheRenegadeMama.com/collections/frontpage /products/copy-of-kids-positive-affirmation-cards.

Peace Out, a podcast from bedtime.fm, offers story-based guided meditation and yoga for kids. Bedtime.fm/peaceout.

The Whole Brain Child by Daniel J. Siegel and Tina Payne Bryson explains, with plenty of examples, how children's brains work and how that manifests in their behavior.

Greg Santucci is an occupational therapist who shares helpful resources to explain what's underneath behaviors. Facebook.com /gregsantucciOT.

Ross Greene has written several books that can help you work with your child to find a mutual solution. More information can be found at LivesInTheBalance.org.

INDEX

ABOUT THE AUTHOR

 **Stacy Spensley** is a coach, author, podcast host, and teacher who supports parents with self-care and survival strategies to help them thrive. She's the founder of Semi-Crunchy Mama®, where she provides resources to help parents feel more confident in their parenting decisions, from birth preparation and breastfeeding, to talking about social justice, inclusivity, and equity issues with our children. She's also active in the San Diego birth and parenting community. Stacy spends most of her time feeding her three children, reading voraciously, and sighing deeply. You can find her work at SemiCrunchyMama.com.